Streaming Life
A
Poetic
Journey

Robert E. Paletz

Copyright© 2021 by Robert E. Paletz

Manufactured in the United States of America

All rights reserved. No part of this book may be used, stored or reprinted in any system or manner whatsoever without written permission from the author, except in cases of reprints in the context of articles and reviews.

Email personal comments to: rpaletz@hotmail.com

Book design and interior illustrations by: BlumeDesign
www.LaurieBlume.com

Introduction & Acknowledgments

Dear Family and Friends,

In addition to a life of work and raising a family, I was fortunate enough to also find some special time to write poetry.

The motivation to write poetry came from a desire to make my life, and the lives of others, happier and more fulfilling with words and thoughts that could touch hearts and stir feelings of well-being. I sincerely hope this is what you will experience from reading my book, *Streaming Life: A Poetic Journey*.

I want to thank my wife Susan for encouraging me for many years to publish this book. She has always been -- and continues to be -- the guiding force in my writing career.

A special thank you goes out to my graphic designer and book illustrator Laurie Blume of BlumeDesign.

Also, a big thank you to my dear friends Charles and Dawn Verhey for their assistance with pre-print production.

And for the blessings of family, thank you to Libby, Matthew, Jacob and Evan Welch … Matthew, Amanda, Grant and Samuel Paletz … and to my sisters Rhoda Werblin and Sheila Spector who have always been there for me … and finally, to my parents Gladys and Samuel Paletz, of blessed memory, who instilled in me a love of words, verse and poetry.

Warmest regards with love to all,

Robert E. Paletz

March, 2021

We

we look
we like
we wonder

we dream
we think
we meet

we kiss
we touch
we love

we cry
we regret
we rejoice

and hope we are …

Foresee

so much a stranger
yet so much a friend
and so we cannot help
but probe in the past
for beginnings
or in the present
for an end
to barriers that
must be there
how else can one
be free
to reach out and touch
without touching
and then have
the courage
to be
so much a stranger
yet so much a friend

Friendship

Newfound friendship.
Warmed by the glow of
light refracted through
a shared prism of
pain and pleasure,
traveling at
the speed of life
through past experiences,
present challenges
and future dreams.

Simple. Beautiful. Exciting.
To bond with strangers.
To enjoy their animation
and attractiveness
in the space of time
so short ...
and to come away with
an emerging friendship
whose small purpose is
to love the desire
to make our lives
more complete.

Self Image

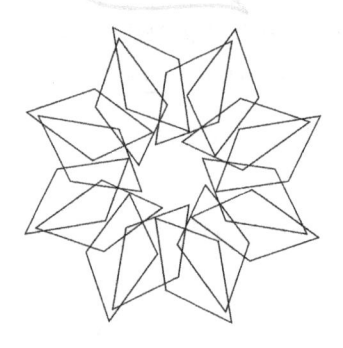

You. Yes. You.
It's okay.
Don't look away.
Look into the
mirror of your mind.

Whatever negative image
you may see, remember
that it is filtered through
a hazy and shadowed lens
that focuses on the
pain and fear of coming
into the light of a positive
and pleasing existence.

You. Yes. You.
Look now.
Look often.
And declare to
the world at large:

I am here.
I am loved.
I am me.

Gone

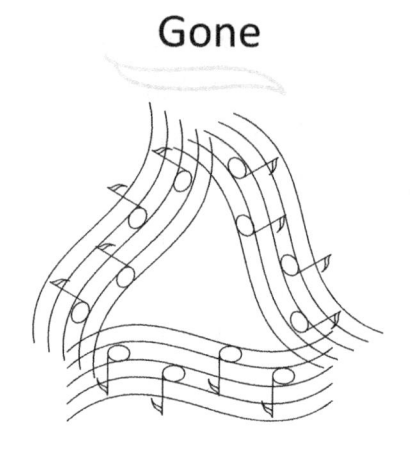

After I am gone
come visit
my grave
once in a while.

But please —
No tears.
No mourning.
Just dance.

Dance to the
Music of memory.

Dance to the
Rhythm of remembering:

Unabated laughter.
Unfettered fun.
Unabridged joy.
Unbounded love.

Meredith

It was an unnatural thing to do,
but winter did not care, and selfishly
eloped with spring late one March leaving
only a premature summer to dry unseasonal tears.

But delicate days masquerading as real summer
were not up to the task and faltered badly.
Its trappings of warmth ... and sun ... and flowers
could not fully nurture the void
that suddenly was there.

Winter's cruel hiatus would soon be over and
spring's debut could not be delayed indefinitely,
but how to regain our emotional balance when
grief and anger played together so intimately upon
the chaotic green?

The shinning eyes. The sweet tuft of hair.
The giving smile. The well of happiness.
Child of time in a place where none of us
wanted to be, your precious being makes warmth
welcome again ... and gives us hope that hearts
broken may soon mend, and that the seasons will
once again evolve in their natural order.

Dog Bailey

Sweet mother earth
warm his tender body
from the chill of death
and the cold of fall and
winter ever so near.

Kiss his gentle heart
with the dew of tears
that tumble from the clouds,
and from our eyes that can
see him now only in
memory's mirror.

Shelter him always
In the rush of sun-kissed mornings
and in the calm of star-filled nights
so that we, the living, can find
peace of mind in knowing
that his new, earthly home
is truly a place of eternal comfort.

Susan

Enough of story and tale
which come, of course, from a loving heart,
for you are my truth, my start in life:
take the cup, lift the veil.

The pledge is sounded in your gaze,
rhapsody, rhapsody in a single note,
what writer, poet, composer wrote
more heartfelt music in his days?

None, sir, do the masses state,
and rightly so is love's reply
to those who would rear their heads and try
to undo the timeless mate.

So walk with me in sunlight,
let moonlight touch your eye,
never to wipe the tear from cry
that ever our love would be undone.

A Chocolate Square

So tempting, so delicious,
it summons my taste buds to dare.

That I should be so lucky
as to partake of a morsel so fair.

And with the joy of consuming,
a challenge to my inner nature is laid bare.

I must make a momentous decision:
To share – or not to share?!

Warm Being

The hour has turned to morning,

an early morning somewhere

in the warmth of life.

Night's legacy, the dark, hovers.

Diffused. Serene.

Hush. Listen.

The sunless air pauses to yawn

and then scurries about its

pre-dawn tasks.

And in this special somewhere

a being ... warm ... sleeps sound.

Thinking

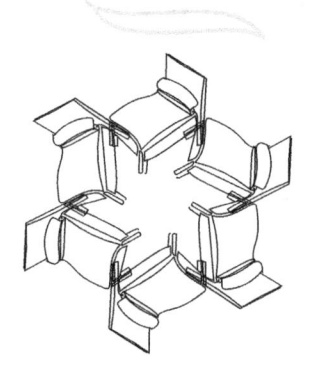

I thought about you.
Last night.
Late.

Long after day had succumbed
to night's advances and slipped
between sheets of earthly green
under the covers of loving darkness.

What a dynamic relationship:

> Radiant day with her splendid sun,
> teasing and taunting with searing heat,
> shear foreplay until dusk when the
> horizon becomes her welcomed bed.

> Exuberant night with his super stars,
> glowing and touching with sensuous light,
> until the darkness is fully spent,
> their union firm, their course complete.

I thought about you.
Last night.
Late.

Long after day had succumbed
to night's advances.
There is so much joy in thinking ...

Caroline

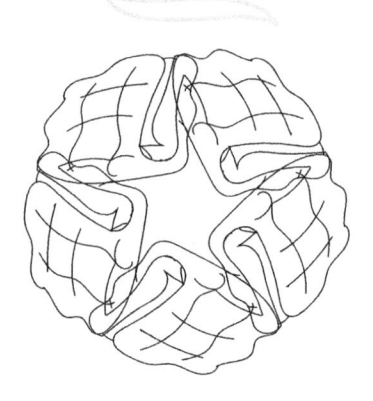

We
really don't know
ourselves
or each other
until forces
beyond our control
encircle us
in spheres
of uncertainty.

Instinctively
our hearts
return to the past
our minds
collide with the present
and our souls
dance in the future.

We desperately need
the music
of our existence
to play forever
and to know
without having to ask
that love is
the true lyric
of our lives.

Competition

The triumphant sun of a
thousand fields,
its nipples turgid in
the gasping earth
rushes at day's end to find
solace there ...

The resplendent moon o'er an
eager sea,
its beams lithe to
the ebbing tide,
seeks with urgent lips to kiss
the sweetness there ...

The exuberant stars of an
endless sky
their attire brilliant in
the space-filled night,
strive relentlessly to reflect
the love there ...

The Sun.
The Moon.
The Stars.

Nature's children
each competing in their natural state
for recognition there ...

Awed by their universal power,
it is not strange for a solitary soul to query:
who, but for a god, could compete with them
for a place there ... in your eyes?

50th Wedding Anniversary

Yes ...
I can see it now.
Through the haze of life.
The clarity is quite remarkable.

The years glow:
Children.
Grandchildren.
Extended family.

Our journey will end.
Our journey will begin again.
Take my hand.

Focus.
Together.
Forever.

Elizabeth Ann

Not just another smile
   Only beaming to please:
But a light, lasting ...
   Warming us to ease.

Not just another heart
   Merely beating to live:
But a source, surging ...
   Inspiring us to give.

Not just another voice
   Clamoring loudly to release:
But a dove, soaring ...
   Leading us to peace.

Not just another mind
   Simply questioning above:
But a force, flowing ...
   Nurturing us to love.

   Heaven of Woman.
   Earth of Man.
   Child of God.
   Elizabeth Ann.

Muse Magic

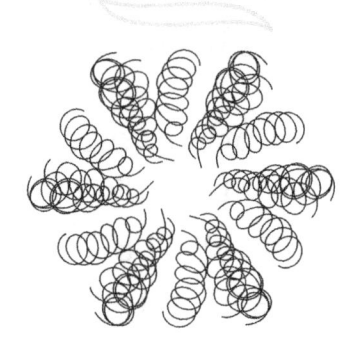

it stirs at odd hours
often times without warning
moving swiftly
surging with so much power
that we can scarcely keep up
leaving us breathless
yet utterly fulfilled

knowing that we share
this emotion-laden friend
and respond to its
awesome mind-mischief
without regard to
time or space
seals forever
our special bond
with muse magic

Cinq

It had to be done.
Your way.
The only way.

Complex.
Simple.

Hard.
Easy.

Up.
Down.

Stress.
Release.

Good.
Bad.

Tears.
Smiles.

Support.
Love.

Setbacks.
Victories.

Four point.
Success.

It had to be done.

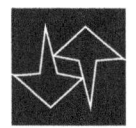

Decisions

Directions.
Choices.
Decisions.

The winds of change can be warm,
or suddenly cold at the height of love's velocity.

Gentle rains can kiss a cheek softly,
or turn it raw with nature's tears.

Dreams at birth continue to be born,
and letting go is not succumbing to their end.

Nurturing.
Caring.
Molding.

Loving.
Dreaming.
Hoping.

Life's precious minutes grant each of us
but mere seconds for ...

Directions.
Choices.
Decisions.

Matthew

Hey Gingerbread man
Who's the power

Maybe it's a lion
king of the jungle

It's a chancy job
and it makes a man
watchful and a little
lonely

Jolting
John

Young Man
Old Radio

Freberg.
I appreciate it
I appreciate it

Well it matters
to the sheep

Pot
Belly
Forty

Walk down the hill
Because the cat was never in the cradle.

All my love forever ... Dad

Sweaters

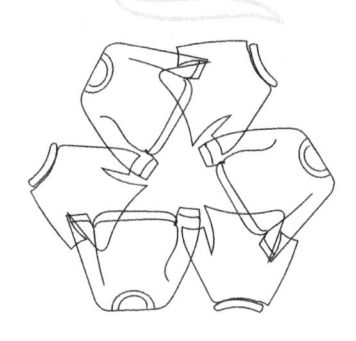

sweaters
blue

you
wear
mine

i
wear
yours

by accident
or on purpose

the reason
is not important

what matters is
the knit of love

Raindrops

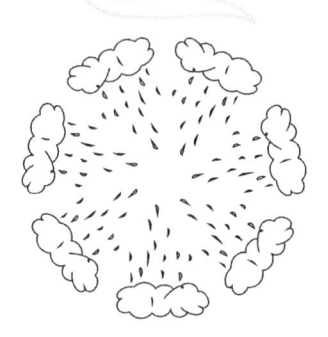

Is it the sun sweating
or the moon perspiring?

Is it the sun laughing
or the clouds dancing?

Is it the angels weeping
or God crying?

Who has time to think
when walking between
raindrops?

Jacob

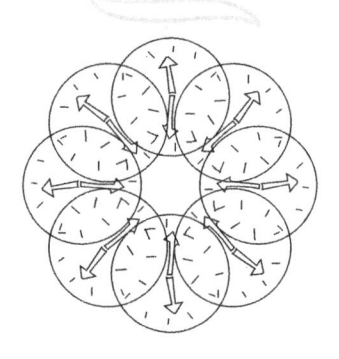

Twenty-nine minutes
before the mid of night
on a willing Thursday
twenty days into July
in two zero zero six
you
Mr. Jacob Martin Welch
decided
it was time to see the world.

Warm night.
Cool birth.
Super parents.
Lucky you.
A labor of love.
Then.
Now.
Forever.

Love,
Z

Evan

Just when you think all the
Places in your heart are taken,
Along comes someone very special.
And through the magic of love
As much room as needed
Is created immediately.

The heart is so expansive.
And for good reason.
You never know when a new life
Needs room in an old heart.

And so, Evan Welch, I have taken
You into my heart and you can
Stay there forever.
I will do all I can so that you
Will never want to leave.

Love,
Z

Grant

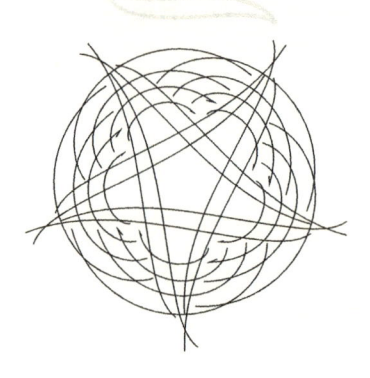

As I cuddle your gentle form
in the early months of your being,
I feel the pulse of the future
in you, Grant Paletz ...
It is strong and vibrant and secure.

As your tiny fingers grip my aging hand,
a lifelong bond is set in motion.
We will soar together
rising above matters of little merit,
and discover special rainbows
on the high plain.

Our journey will be blessed with sunlight,
and should rain clouds mist our way
I pledge to you a clear path of love
going straight to my heart forever.

Love,
Z

Samuel

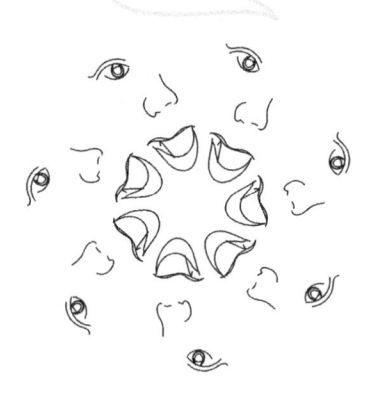

Dearest Samuel Paletz,
A
Legacy
Of
Love
Is
Transmitted in your smile.

A
Smile
So
Bright
That it reaches the horizon of my heart.

A
Smile
So
Warm
That it evokes thoughts of future dreams.

A
Smile
So
Lasting
That it cradles my being and
ensures a good name.

Love,
Z

Sela

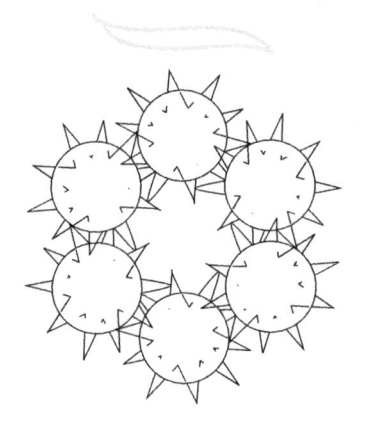

We
have
bonded
in
a precious world of love
that transcends the present
and soars to a future
filled with dreams fashioned
by the sunlight in your smile.

I
am
a
grandfather
not yours by birth
but surely by mirth
knowing that your happiness
and well-being will be on my mind
and in my heart forever.

Love,
Zayde Bob

Complex / Simple

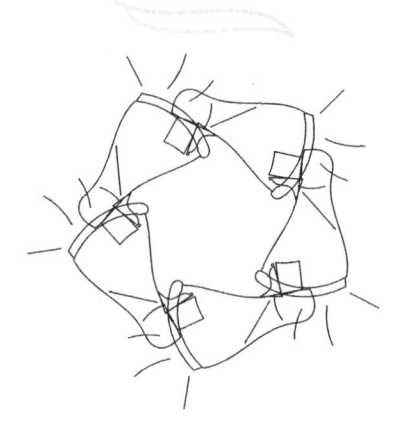

In a world gone crazy
by the complexities
of all things simple ...

when one's spirit and
soul are challenged
by vexations
from all corners of
our lives ...

and when we attempt
to change the course
of the human gyroscope
that daily spins out
of control ...

we lose our breath
and sometimes our will
to find the one moment,
the one second that we
can truly call our own ...

and in that one moment,
in that one second, a voice
young but strong breaks
through the din and gives
us a glimmer of hope
and love ... a voice that gives
us the emotional fuel we need
to keep our dreams alive and
make ourselves whole.

Legacy

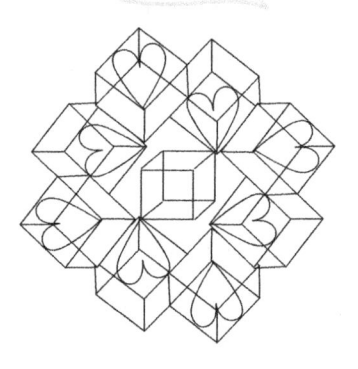

We are a family
blessed beyond the stars.

Endless faith,
or random fate?

It matters not the cause
of our earthly union
but the purpose ... love.

Love ... within and beyond
the borders of what we have
been taught from birth until now.

We are here and the open plains
of emotion beckon us to journey
over common and uncommon ground.

To bond and to build something
so special that destiny's arms
will embrace:

>	our loved ones from the past,
>	our loved ones in the present,
>	our loved ones of the future,
>	and insure to us all
>	a legacy of love.

A Prayer On Thanksgiving

Dear God in the heavens,

Thank you for the gift of our lives.

And for this day of Thanksgiving and rest
so that we may share the food of your earth
with all those who are near and dear to us.

Thank you for the power to remember,
and to love those who have touched our
lives in the past and in the present.

Thank you for the opportunity to hope,
through prayer and acts of kindness, that
our world will one day soon be at peace.

Bless our troops who guard our freedom
and bless our family with good health and safety.

And let us say Amen.

Thanksgiving

Dearest God in the heavens
Our prayers this Thanksgiving Day
Are not for more – but to do more.
In the words of the prophet Micah:
"What do you Lord require of us?
To Act Justly
To Love Mercy
To Walk Humbly
In Your Sight."
We pray and pledge to protect
The bounty of your earth
And to always share it lovingly with others.

To love.
To peace.
To life.

L'Chayim
And let us all say … Amen.

Dillon

Waiting
Not an option
For Dillon
The time is now
To find his mountain
To climb it with courage
Adventure beckons
The road of life responds
His journey is his resume
To be written by the
Twists and turns and
The ups and downs of his trek
Read it and rejoice
For this is his true path
His destiny unfolding along the way
Fulfilling dreams
Shaping tomorrow
Creating the future

Elana

Finding her skies.
Here.
There.
Everywhere.
Reaching out.
Drawing in.
With her mind.
With her hands.
With her heart.
With her soul.
Finding good.
Challenging bad.
Seeking truth.
Fighting lies.
Always in motion.
Traveling through life
At the speed of love.

Izabela

To dance.
So complex.
Yet so simple.

A cross-body lead
from mind and heart
to the core of
your creativity.

A frame of style.
A profile of beauty.
A line of direction.

To teach.
To inspire.
To perform.

To strive.
To compete.
To achieve.

Highly skilled instructor.
Eager, anxious student.

Bonding to the rhythmic
and elusive task of
reaching for the stars
in the dance of life.

Joan

Dearest Joan,

Paths cross ...

People bond ...

Relationships form ...

Families emerge ...

Happiness endures ...

And it all started because of you.

How can we ever thank you enough?

Perhaps with prayers ... kind words ... and

Much love.

Happy 70th Birthday!

Colorado Vistas

Life-affirming sunlight
leaps unafraid from peaks
of towering mountains,
through clouds moist and anxious,
kissing the eager tree line
as it falls into the loving arms
of glorious foothills.

Beautiful sun take your leave
for night is on its way.
The moon seeks out all tides.
The stars are restless to shine.

Come first light of morning
the miracle of day begins anew,
with dazzling sunlight filling
the mountainous heavens above.

And through the power
of this daily, illuminating journey,
we are blessed with the clarity to
marvel once again at the wonders of
precious life, sweet love and
enduring friendship.

Lisa

Lisa Hope, precious niece,
    Cuddled in your blanket warm.
The night is day, bright with love
    Of your gentle form.

Stir – and you mesmerize us.
    Our words fail but our thoughts elope
To count all the dreams you fulfill,
    Happiness always, Lisa Hope.

Lynne

Somewhere
along the fault line
of your life,
in the hidden forest
of secret emotions,
the crashing sound of
personal timbers
echoes unabated
in the dark,
negative night.

But come dawn,
each new day is filled
with the positive energy
of mind and body,
fueled by love from
spouse, family and friends,
to help you renew your spirit,
to keep you in the fight,
to see you win the battle
to become whole again.

Claire

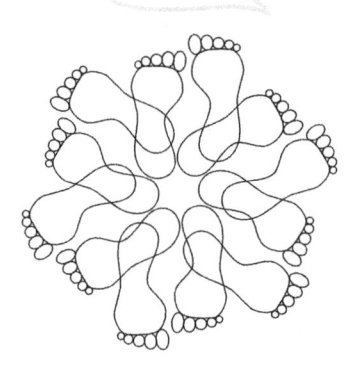

Rhythms of the night
enhance the melody
of a newborn's day,
accompanying and
safeguarding its
wondrous journey
through space and time
under suns golden
and stars silvery blue.

Listen carefully:
  Soft breath.

Look gently:
   Sweet countenance.

Love soars and the heart
follows without hesitation,
and the echo of precious
footsteps is forever
in the dance of a new life.

Chance

Chance – a time frame
    as brief as a glance.
A beat – a second
    for minds to dance.
To embrace all-knowing,
    to know nothing at all.
Surging to the rhythm of
    life's masquerade ball.

The time is short
    for our masks to fall.
Scars may be there,
    harsh memories to recall.
You took that step
    while time yearned to advance.
And in that second
    I believed in chance.

If

If I am happy,
Do not question this right;
Let me be the judge
Of what is delight.

And if I am bitter,
Do not question this right;
For mortals who judge
See without sight.

Together

Dusk
played restlessly
upon the blinds
its fidgeting light
now
only
half
perceived
as we talked
softly into the
hour.

Silence
at times
to reflect perhaps
upon a darkened
path
then
words
again
and light anew
full of warmth
in being
together.

Hearts

Hearts volunteering to be soft
in a hard-hearted world
deserve much recognition.

For having the courage to beat.
Hey world, we believe in our
pairing and in ourselves.

Caution:
Actions can hurt.
Words can wound.

Trust
our hearts.

Look
to love.

Look
no further.

Light & Crystal

Deep within the recesses
of soft dark harmonies
a restless light gathers speed,
and with atonal force
penetrates the static crystal.

The wake is stunning: in a flash
the refractive specter is gone,
its clarifying presence
just a millisecond of
fleeting fantasies.

Relationships

True
relationships
require
a
hard-core
commitment.

Soothing
emotions
when
the
truth
hurts.

Being
there
when
life
is
painful.

Securing
ties
when
bonds
fray.

Letting
love
in
and
keeping
it
warm.

Sparks

The space of our lives
draws sustenance from
Time:
    Seconds to embrace.
    Minutes to believe.
    Hours to reflect.

Our lives found a space
in the present
Light:
    Glaring with passion,
    Blazing with pleasure.
    Glowing with restraint.

Our time was a space
for just a
Spark:
    Giving us hope.
    Keeping us whole.
    Helping us live.

Time

Time is the loving sister of fate,
    Comforting the brother who is lost,
When his sea is coarse and turbulent,
    His ship small and tossed.

You will find her there at daybreak
    Guarding him from onrushing fears.
She sleeps not the night – there is need.
    To kiss away his tears.

The Sun

a rumor
not to be believed
until I experienced
the phenomenon
first hand

the sun had
lost its warmth
and had become even
more distant from my
earthly being

others spoke out
you must be crazy
yes I replied
I must be crazy
to want the warmth
of the sun
to feel its loving rays as
I age to the grave

but I still have hope
that one day soon
the sun will find
its warmth again --
and seek my waiting heart

Patricia

A long life
suddenly can
seem so short,
especially when
the eternal caretaker
pays an unwelcomed
visit and leaves a
painful void
among the living.

In the grief of the day
through tears and sorrow,
your steps forward
will not falter
if you dance
in the light of memory
and remember
her beauty ...
her style ...
her grace ...
and find comfort always
in the warmth of her love.

Molly

a gentle mount
a rough trail
a long ride
a ride cut short

pastures of pain
corrals of caring
fields of faith
paths of prayers

questions loom
answers hide
tight reins
steady gallop

on and on
you must go
end of the road
just the beginning

lead with courage
look forward with hope
live your purpose
love away the tears

A Perfect Day

A perfect day
in a serene park
with two special friends
seeking new answers
to old questions
about disturbing politics
and deadly pandemics.

But through it all
in the dazzling sunlight
on the luscious green
with a gentle breeze
we did our collective best
to calm our anxious hearts.

No matter what may come
our abiding friendship
will sustain us forever
with the love
that brought us together
on a perfect day
in a serene park.

Rhoda / Sheila

And so
here we are ...
maturing shells
on the beach of life
enjoying the warmth
of a nurturing sun
and the cooling tone
of rushing waves.

A long way
from cold country
but so close
with warm sibling hearts
that have always
been there for each other.

A journey of love
that has only begun
because the beach
is endless ... with
much more life sand
to be refined.

106

Made in the USA
Coppell, TX
04 November 2024